THE HOME GUARD

Hints for the Home Guard

Training and Duties ; Including the Methods of Defeating an Armed Man

OBSERVATION
COMMUNICATION
SELF-PRESERVATION

by

Lieut.-Col. DUNCAN C. L. FITZWILLIAMS

C.M.G., M.D., CH.M., F.R.C.S.

30th Thousand

Published in Great Britain in 2013 by Old House books & maps,
Midland House, West Way, Botley, Oxford OX2 0PH, United Kingdom.
4301 21st Street, Suite 220B, Long Island City, NY 11101, USA.
Website: www.oldhousebooks.co.uk

A CIP catalogue record for this book is available from the British Library
ISBN-13: 978 1 90840 272 1
Originally published c.1940 by Hutchinson & Co Ltd, London.
Printed in China through Worldprint Ltd.

13 14 15 16 17   10 9 8 7 6 5 4 3 2 1

INTRODUCTION

This small pamphlet was written with the idea of collecting hints which would prove useful to those who were joining what was then called the Local Defence Force and is now styled the Home Guard and who had had little training or experience in scouting, observing or resisting an enemy.

Through the kindness of my old chief, Sir Edmund Ironside, now a Field Marshal, the pamphlet was corrected by an officer detailed by General Pownall, the Inspector of the Local Defence Force. This officer and one from the staff of the Director of Military Training corrected it and added many valuable suggestions. To all these officers I tender my grateful thanks.

The work is very incomplete as the duties of the force are still ill-defined and are rapidly increasing in number and importance. I have not touched on certain important points, such as the work of the Home Guard on estuaries, waterways, fen and marsh lands, along the coast line, or in towns. All these areas have special problems of their own.

Section Commanders in these districts are asked to be kind enough to send me their views on the special points of their work. In this way a more helpful guide may appear in future editions.

My grateful thanks for many useful hints are rendered to Major Maurice Beachcroft, Battalion Commander, Eastern Division of Bucks; to Captain Charles, the second in Command of the Bray Company, and Lieutenant Robbins, in Command of the Bray Platoon.

45 PARK STREET,
LONDON, W.1

CONTENTS

STATUS

The Home Guard are members of His Majesty's forces and therefore have military rights and obligations. They are subject to military law when carrying out their duties. Being forces of the Crown, they have the duty of dealing with the King's enemies in any manner they find necessary. They may arrest and detain all suspected persons. These they will hand over to the Authorities, or inform the Authorities of the arrest within 24 hours.

The importance of the Home Guard is fully recognized by the Authorities, and the Inspector-General of the Home Guard is Lieut.-General H. R. Pownall, who was chief of staff to Lord Gort. He in turn is under the War Office, and works in the closest contact with the C.-in-C. of the Home Forces.

The Home Guard are divided up into Battalions, Companies, Platoons, and Sections The Battalion is 1,000 to 1,200 men, the Company 400, the Platoon 100, the Section 25, and the Patrol 6 or 7 men. Each Section has an area of the country under its control. Each Section has a Section Commander, on whom falls the duty of training and commanding the members of his Section. He is, therefore, a very important person in the organization, for on him rests the responsibility for the efficiency of the body of the force.

The Home Guard are the best defence against the Fifth Columnist. They know the locality, and are the best able to guide and assist the Military in the absence of all direction signs. They know the inhabitants and their occupations, and whether so-and-so should be out at night or not. They know a stranger. Anything they note as suspicious should be reported to the Section Commander and by him to the police.

As the force is new, its organization will take some time to complete and develop. Patience will be needed ; help, not criticism, is asked for from all. Arms are being supplied as quickly as possible, but it will be some time before every man has a weapon.

Section Commanders will have plenty to do in organizing

and training their Sections, and the members will have plenty to learn. The enrolment of the Section may even take some time. As the Force is voluntary, the more that join the less often will each one have to go on duty and give up part of his night's rest. Much training can be undertaken which does not necessitate the bearing of weapons.

Training and organization will gradually go forward and all should help in any way they can. We must learn to walk before we learn to run. Impatience never helps : keenness, on the other hand, does.

Time may be short, so all our energies should be expended in rendering ourselves as efficient as possible.

The Section hut is not, as a rule, luxuriously furnished. Often it is a barn, a disused garage, or a draughty shed. Nevertheless, an effort should be made to make it as comfortable as possible. Much can be done with little expense. The neighbours are the members of the Section, and they can often lend or give things, such as a lantern, an oil stove for making tea, some chairs, a table, or a dart board. Old curtains are useful to black out the windows and to keep out draughts.

The local carpenter, or someone fond of carpentry, should rig up bunks round the walls.

Storage of Arms

Many of the Section will have, or be supplied with, sporting guns. Cartridges loaded with ball or buckshot will be provided. Guns should not be left lying about on tables, in bunks or in odd corners, or strangers will certainly handle them and accidents may occur. Racks should be provided, not one, but two or more in different parts of the hut. All the guns should never be placed in one rack. If there is a gun in one rack. the next man should place his gun in another rack. There will be less confusion if they are needed in a hurry, and the risk of an undesirable getting between the patrol and their firearms is diminished.

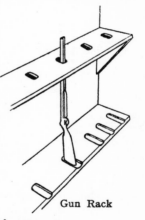

Gun Rack

Pens, ink, and paper—including carbon paper—should be available for messages.

Other details will probably be arranged by the Section Commander and the members themselves.

Notices

Full information on the following points should be posted in the hut.

1. Names, addresses, and occupations of the Section members, so that they may know about each other.

2. The duties of each member should be clearly stated.

  (a) Ordinary routine duties.
  (b) On emergency.

3. The Alarm—who should sound it, and how?

4. The rendezvous or rallying point where the members should collect immediately the alarm is sounded; other rallying points if the one mentioned is captured.

5. The local Police Headquarters—address and 'phone number.

6. Observation or road defence posts. These should be mentioned, and who should go to each. How they will go, whether by motor, cycle or on foot. This is important, as messages have to be sent back. The situation of the post should be clearly indicated. A notice, for instance, "Rendezvous No. 3", in large letters near the important cross roads.

7. How communication with the different parts of the Section is to be maintained.

8. Headquarters, its address and 'phone number. Everyone should know the situation of headquarters and how to get there by road, or by path across the fields should the roads be blocked.

Warning

A warning should be posted about taking orders from a stranger, whether in uniform or not, especially about abandoning a post or retreating. The person giving the order should be known to the recipient. All orders will naturally be given to the Section Commander. If they are handed to a Section member to give to his leader they should be suspect, especially verbal orders given by unknown people who hurry away.

Local Maps

Many members of the Home Guard have been town dwellers but now live in dormitory towns round the large cities. The town dweller knows that every street has a name and each house a number. He knows that in the country every village, house and farm has its name; but he may not realize that this applies also to every feature of the countryside, and that every mountain, hill, valley, wood, stream, lake, pond, road, lane, quarry, and many fields, all possess their own names. Unlike the names in towns those in the country never change, and those mentioned in Domesday Book are substantially the same to-day. An ordnance map should be kept in the hut. It contains all the local names, and the members of the Section should study it. This map should be locked up, or hidden, when not in use.

THE SECTION : THE COMMANDER

Each Section has a Commander. In many cases he is an officer or soldier who has served either in the last war or, better still, in the Boer War, where he will have picked up many points in scouting and craftsmanship.

He can teach his Section much. Many of them will never have handled firearms and will need schooling in their use. Many of the Sections may consist of young cadets too youthful for calling up and all keen to learn ; many will have useful knowledge of a sporting gun.

The drilling of the men should be undertaken systematically, and if an old Sergeant-Instructor can be obtained so much the better. If he is not up-to-date and does not know the rifle issued, he can go to the nearest Barracks and ask for a day's instruction. Even instructors get rusty. Opportunities for practice firing can be made with the nearest rifle range.

The Section Commander should know his Section and their families personally.

No man other than an enrolled Home Guard will be allowed to do duty with the Section.

The Section Commander should direct the attention of his Section to the points laid down for compass-reading at night, and the various points mentioned under the heading of night work. Unless attention is directed to these points they are apt to be overlooked.

The Commander should keep a log-book in the Section hut and note anything of interest mentioned by his Section. He should encourage each member of his Section to take a pocket book to write down what he has noted during his hours of duty. Some of his Section may be seniors who may not take kindly to these suggestions, but with tact, and as an example to the younger members, they may be persuaded to accept them.

This all smacks very much of the boy-scouts movement, but I know of no better rules and regulations on which to model a Section, and former boy-scouts should make invaluable members of Sections or Section Commanders.

The Commander should get as many of the Section as he can to give verbal or written reports to him as they come off duty. In this way they will become proficient in imparting knowledge without undue verbiage, so that information may be passed on clearly.

A Commander can test his men's powers of observation by asking them casual questions about the area as if he desired information such as the distance between two points in the area and the shortest way to get from one to the other ; or, if the church steeple is north or west of Dovecote Farm. In various ways he can add interest to work which otherwise is apt to become boring. Duty on a wet night is a poor job.

Strangers

The Section must expect strangers from time to time and those who know members of the Section will probably be welcomed. But there will also be strangers who are not known to members of the Section, or who say they are friends of members of the Section who are out on duty, none of those present being able to vouch for them. This situation may be very difficult, and strangers should not be welcomed indiscriminately. A common way of picking up an acquaintance is for the Home Guard on patrol to find a man leaning on a gate, and, having nothing to do on patrol, to start a conversation with him, when by judicious questioning the man may find out many things about the other members of the Section. A few evenings later, he may fall in with his acquaintance and walk with him to the Section hut, and so come in under his patronage. Undesirables may thus quite easily gain access to the Section hut, and later, it will be very difficult to say who introduced them.

There is quite a large section of countrymen who are early risers, such as cowmen, dairy farmers, vegetable pickers, etc., who might be a valuable adjunct to the Section.

The Section Commander would do well to get in touch

with such people, and instructions as to informing the police if they see anything suspicious, might be given to them.

The Section Commander will have a very mixed lot under his charge. Some will be intelligent enough to learn with rapidity, others will have a very slow mentality. There are three essentials, therefore, that should be impressed upon them all from the first—other details can follow later—they are, OBSERVATION, COMMUNICATION and SELF-PRESERVATION. Most of the remarks on Sections come under one of these heads.

Defence of the Area

All Section Commanders should be informed :

1. As to the general plan of the defence of the district.
2. What is to happen if one or more posts are captured.
3. Where casualties are to be sent and how ?

Blocking Roads

If it is the duty of the Home Guard to block roads, it will be the Section Commander's duty to supervise this. He will have to see that the material is kept ready and not removed for any purpose. He should rehearse the procedure to see that there is no hitch and that the material is sufficient for the purpose. He should satisfy himself that there is no way by lane or path to evade the obstruction.

Neighbouring Sections

It is advisable to know as much as possible about neighbouring Sections and if possible the members should meet and try to get to know one another. They will be meeting on the confines of their districts at night and should have some means of recognizing each other, perhaps by sign and counter sign. If this is not done, they may spend their time spying on each other.

THE SECTION: NIGHT WORK

As sections work chiefly at night they should know something about the night. Those who live in the country have unconsciously absorbed knowledge which is quite strange to the boy or young man brought up in an Urban district. It has been said that the chief astonishment of a town child on going to the country is the falling of night. In towns the shops light up at dusk and the child never sees darkness all round him.

People may at first find night life in the country strange, but they will soon get used to it. Many things are different at night, and have different values, distances appear greater, certain landmarks scarcely noticed during the day stand out at night. Everything is quieter but you seem to make more noise, you stumble more as you move, you cannot see where to tread, what loose stone to avoid, or what puddle to miss.

Your senses take a different value ; in the day you depend on your eyes mostly to tell you things, but in the night it is your ears which are most important, and occasionally your nose. For instance, as you go quietly up a lane walking on the grassy side, as you should to avoid noise, there may be a man in the gate fifty yards further up whom you cannot see, and as he is still you do not hear ; but if the wind is towards you and he is smoking you should know of his presence.

Knowledge of Your Section Area

This is invaluable if you are to work with any comfort and it involves a little trouble. You had better go over your area in the day time. The things to note are very many. I can only give a few here, but they will serve to illustrate my meaning. Naturally, they will vary in different parts of the country. There is little in common between the downs of Sussex, the wild hills of Scotland, Wales or Yorkshire, and the hedges and ditches of the cattle-raising countries, or even with the market-garden areas round the towns.

Make yourself familiar with your own boundaries ; know all the roads, lanes and paths in your area and where they lead. Ascertain, by means of map and compass, in which direction they run and where to ; what is their importance, and whether they are short-cuts to anywhere.

Know every gateway ; which are locked, which creak on opening, which open easily and silently ; every stile and how to get over them in the dark, say, with a bicycle.

Know the best view-points, especially those to the East as the sun goes down, and in the West as it rises. A rifle or bayonet may reflect the sun's rays and betray the presence of an enemy.

Learn the outlines of the chief buildings as they are seen at night from different angles, such as churches, farms or public houses. It is wise to see the silhouette of these places while lying on the ground. Remember that if you are ever going to make use of your knowledge it will be at a time when you want cover and you will then be lying flat.

Be careful to look back in strange country. It is by looking back that you can retrace your steps to where you started from. When returning, you will be looking at the other side of objects you passed as you went out. You cannot recognize that view if you have not looked back and seen it. Therefore get into the habit of looking back.

Ascertain the nearest telephone to the far end of your beat, it may be nearer than the Section hut, or the enemy may be between you and the hut.

Post offices and telephones are especially important as those are the places to which Fifth Column men will go to direct troops and to give false orders and information. Houses with 'phones are distinguished by the wire going to them. Note suitable cover round them for observation and where a possible field of fire for your particular weapon may be obtained.

It is wise to note what is the nature of the hedges, whether prickly or not, where there is a hole through which you can pass quickly—a prickly hedge is a formidable obstacle at night to a stranger.

If in open country, note where the banks or walls can be seen against the sky-line.

Taking Cover

The wearing of the magic cloak of invisibility is invaluable to the patrol man. He should learn how to put it on, t is very easy.

Dress. This is important. The clothes, naturally, will be old ones till uniform is provided. They should be of a dark or nondescript colour. If coat, trousers, breeches and stockings are all of different colours or shades, so much the better, they will merge better with any background.

If you are in greenish-brown clothes you will merge with the same coloured background, a hedge, a cultivated field, or a shady place. Be careful, if you are standing in shade under a tree, that you are not showing up strongly against the sunlit field beyond the tree. Shade is not background ;

background is what the other man sees you against. If you are in khaki, the best background is sand, earth, or rocks. Light-coloured clothes, like white flannels or white sweaters, should never be worn at night.

Even on summer nights the air can become very chilly if a person is standing about doing little. Warm clothing is therefore essential to comfort. A dull-coloured cap or close-fitting hat should be worn ; anything like a trilby, straw hat or bowler should be avoided. Thick clothes and a warm pullover, easily fitting, are comfortable. A mackintosh should always be taken, as rain in our climate can always be expected. Most mackintoshes are naturally khaki or brown coloured. White or light-coloured coverings should never be used. Knickerbockers with gaiters or puttees are excellent. Thick woollen socks with boots that allow plenty of room for the feet will keep the feet warm. Good rubber ankle boots can be acquired cheaply. Rubber Wellington boots may be preferred by some, but always seem clumsy. All boots should be watertight. Shoes should not be worn as the grass in the early morning is laden with dew and soaking wet even without rain. In an emergency you may have to lie down and keep low. Here the value of a mackintosh will prove itself. When off duty the coat and pullover can be discarded, but they should be hung up tidily where they can be got at easily in an emergency and in the dark. The boots can be unlaced to ease the feet, or removed and a pair of slippers worn. The boots should always be placed where they are handy ; sometimes in the dark they are difficult to find, especially if there are several pairs about.

Cover. The best cover is immobility. You can walk right on top of a brilliantly coloured cock pheasant and never see him till he suddenly moves. If you keep still and merge with the background, you may need no cover and no one may notice you are there. This is the easier at night when everything blends and all is in semi-shadow.

If you want to see beyond an object, always look round it, never over the top. The top may be on the sky-line to anyone lying flat, and things are most easily noticed against a sky-line. If you have to come over the sky-line keep low and move with extreme slowness. Look round the corner at a gate or a gap, never from the middle.

If you have to look over a wall or a bank, pluck a bunch of grass and put it slowly over the top, then slowly raise your head and look through the grass. In Scotland, the gillies when deer-stalking use a bunch of heather.

If you think your enemy is looking towards you, do not duck down suddenly. Remain quite still ; you may be mistaken for a hummock, a mound, or a rock.

At night, keep close to the ground on every suspicious occasion. You can hear better there, as sound carries along the ground. You are in shadow and anyone moving will be seen against the sky. For this reason, keep to the low ground, get in the ditch, crouch against a bush. When crouching in the shadow of quite a small bush a man can pass within three feet of you and not see you.

Get into the habit of walking quietly ; walk on the grass verge on the side of the road. If you stumble, do not make your usual exclamation.

Observation

It will be as well to say a word on observation and how it is made.

If you watch an expert examine anything and then see the novice do the same, the process is as different as chalk from cheese. The expert feels the thing, rubs it with his fingers to tell its hardness, roughness or smoothness, size and shape, holds it up to the light, weighs it in his hand, smells it, and so on. The novice looks at it and gives it a casual feel, but if you ask him questions later he will say he has not noticed, or will go back to the object to find out. Now, both have used their eyes and fingers ; where, then, was the difference ? Perhaps you do not realize what you examine with. You may, and probably do, think that it is with your eyes, fingers, nose, etc., but it is not. It is your brain that examines things. You brain is unconsciously asking questions which your senses, eyes, ears, fingers answer.

Your brain registers that answer and then you know and can impart the information later. The novice could not impart the information as his brain had never asked the questions, and therefore had registered no answer.

Perhaps you will say, "What rubbish ! I don't agree with all this." But if your attention is distracted and your thoughts far away, you do not see what you are

B

looking at, you do not listen to what is said, you hardly know what you hold in your hand. This is only because your brain is not paying attention and noticing, as we call it. Now you understand the meaning of being alert. It is your brain then that asks the question, and your senses that give the answer. It is for you to train your brain so that it automatically asks the necessary question. Then you will begin to observe things accurately.

Even if you wish to examine a field there is a right way of doing it. If you suspect anyone is in it, do not go through the gate or over a stile if you can avoid doing so. Some-one else may be on the look-out, too. Get through a gap and keep low. Raise the head slowly and look round, never bob your head up and down ; it will attract attention. Try and think where a person in the field would hide.

Pay special attention to :

1. Barns, sheds, haystacks, trees and bushes.
2. Dips in the ground or ditches, along the hedges. That is where people lurk—not in the open.
3. Note if the cattle are feeding quietly. If so, no one is near them. If their heads are all up and all looking in one direction, something is there. If the sheep are huddling or all moving off, it is for the same reason.

It is a good practice for two patrols to go our together —different patrols each night, so that they can exchange ideas and express what they have noticed themselves, or pass on information they have learned from other patrols. In this way a healthy rivalry for observation may be started.

THE SECTION : SIGHTS AND SOUNDS

Although the night is quieter than the day, sound travels much farther and voices can be heard over long distances. It is just as well for members of Sections who work together to have some special call or whistle among themselves. The hoot of an owl repeated so many times is as good as anything. It can be given quietly at those points where you expect to make contact with each other on your rounds.

There are sounds which you must get used to—for instance, the wind in the trees ; this has a different sound in each tree. There are other harmless noises you may hear in the different parts of the country, and if you have a countryman with you to tell you what they are, so much the better. There is the nightingale's song, the hoot or screech of the owls, the sharp short bark of the fox, while among the rarer ones may be the chirr of the nightjar, the scratchy rustling sound of the hedgehog, or the whistle of the otter near a river.

There are certain noises, however, which have a great significance.

The most important of these is the barking of a dog, not the long-drawn-out howl of the dog baying the moon, but the sharp angry bark which denotes that there is something disturbing him—it may be a strange man or it may be a marauding fox. A barking dog is always worth investigating, but be quite sure it is not yourself that has caused the trouble.

The characteristic sharp cackle of cock pheasants in a wood is also most significant and usually means that a man is passing through the wood. As day breaks, the scream of the disturbed jay is most helpful, for the bird will often follow the marauder—man or fox—keeping some way off him and screeching loudly, so that the direction he is making can sometimes be made out.

The sight of a covey of partridges coming over a hedge, or of grouse over the sky-line, may mean that someone has disturbed them.

Something has disturbed that hare which is bolting across the field. What is it? Hares naturally just lope along; they only go full out when disturbed by man or dog.

Any Section man who can arrange to go out with the local keeper should do so, and just as good, but less talked about, is the local ne'er-do-well, or poacher. The amount of animal and nature knowledge these men have is extraordinary, though they are as a rule silent and need drawing out.

Estimation of Numbers from Sound

It is useful to be able to estimate numbers from the sound of footsteps. You may be in hiding and see nothing and yet have a fairly accurate idea of the numbers. It may enable you to prepare to take cover, retreat or to attack. We can all recognize the sound of one man's footsteps, but can you distinguish between two, three, or more ? Try getting members of your Section to walk up and down the road, while some of you are behind the hedge estimating their numbers each time they pass. You will see how often you are correct.

It is difficult to estimate numbers of men marching in step. The Groups or Sections in this case should be counted, and the time each Section takes to pass. In this way a rough estimate can be formed.

For numbers up to twenty or thirty, counting is preferable to estimation. The Home Guard will scarcely have an opportunity of counting enemy lorries, guns or tanks.

There are many things you should note, and for this purpose you should carry a note-book and jot them down. When you come to read it next day you will be reminded of many things you have already forgotten. Do not forget to note any footmarks in the grass. Footsteps in dewy grass are the easiest to follow, but they must be followed before the sun gets hot and dries the grass. They may lead to the house of someone who should not have been out during the night.

Napoleon once said, " 'How' and 'why' cannot be asked too often."

THE SECTION : COMPASS READING

It is most important in giving information, either written or on the 'phone, to be exact in your statements. Thus, if you saw a troop-carrying aeroplane land troops, it would be most useful to report : "Plane landed thirty men dressed in grey, wearing helmets of German shape, at 14.00 hours, half a mile north-east of Jordon's farm ; they were armed with rifles and went into Twoacre Wood." Compare this with a message given, perhaps, by an excited and overwrought but well-meaning person : "I saw a plane land a lot of soldiers a little while ago to the left of the farm on the hill over there ; they all went into the wood. I am sure they are Germans."

One message is to the point, and tells clearly what you want to convey. The other is useless.

To tell the points of the compass during the day, the sun, if seen, can be used. Everyone knows that it rises in the east and sets in the west, and at mid-day it is due south. At night time it is supposed to be more difficult but it is just as easy if the stars are showing.

Our finest constellation goes under various names, such as the Great Bear, the Dipper, the Wain, and the Plough. It consists of seven stars and is readily distinguished. The two end stars are called "the pointers" as they point to the North Star. The Little Bear, which is close by, and very like it on a smaller scale, also consists of seven stars. The end star of the tail is the North Star. Another well-known constellation is Orion and his Belt. It consists of three stars representing his head, one on each side for his

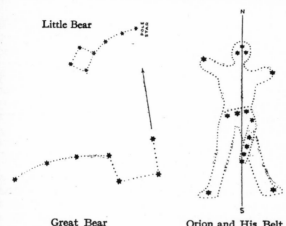

Little Bear

POLE STAR

N

Great Bear   Orion and His Belt

S

shoulders, three stars in a line diagonally across the body for his belt, four hanging down for his sword, and two for his feet. If a line is drawn through his head to the last star of his sword, this line passes due north and south.

These constellations move round as the night advances, but the relative positions always remain the same. No one need be in any doubt as to the points of the compass on a starry night.

It is always wise, however, to mark out in your area two or more marks in line which will give you the points you want even if no stars are showing. The points need not be north and south; they can be east and west, or any intermediate points from which you can calculate.

FIREARMS

Firearms are dangerous weapons. Accidents from their misuse are constantly occurring, not only among those unfamiliar with them, but among those who should know better.

Safeguards

There are certain rules which must be strictly adhered to and enforced by the Section Commander.

1. No firearm should ever be pointed at any person in fun.
2. No one should handle strange firearms except in the presence, and with the permission, of the owner.
3. Anyone taking up a firearm should get into the habit of automatically opening the breech to see if it is loaded. If he does not know how to open the breech, he should lay it down again.
4. No one should ever lay down a firearm which has not been unloaded.

Accidents

If these simple rules were observed there would be fewer accidents. This does not do away with the careless sportsman who walks along with his gun at full cock, who trips and stumbles and whose guns goes off, or who trails it carelessly till a bramble or a branch catches in the trigger and fires it—perhaps into the back of the person in front.

Every person learning to shoot will have the unpleasant experience of having the gun go off unexpectedly. In such cases, he should think out carefully why the accident happened.

In most accidents there are two people responsible for the accident and an unoffending victim. The people responsible are seldom hurt.

This is the gist of the story told again and again in the coroner's court :

A man comes in from shooting and lays down a loaded gun (thereby violating one of the fundamental rules). He is called away. However important the reason for which he is called, he should unload that gun ; it will not take

him five seconds. Two young people come into the room
—they nearly always are young people—and the tempta-
tion is too strong for them. One picks up the gun and, in
a spirit of bravado, says to the other, "Now I will shoot
you." He presses the trigger and his victim falls dead.

With pistols and revolvers the story is much the same.
At the beginning of the last war, a young lieutenant went
to practice with his revolver for the first time. He came
home, laid his revolver on the table, and went to tea. Two
other lieutenants came in. One picked up the revolver
and put his finger in the trigger guard as he held it, hori-
zontally, across his body. It went off and killed the friend
at his side.

The story seldom varies—the two fools and a victim.
A revolver, or pistol, is so short that it is easy to point it
at someone without realizing it. Just watch a person
handling one when he does not know how to use it and
you will realize the truth of this.

Guns and Rifles Compared with Pistols and Revolvers

You get as close to your man as you can with a pistol,
but if with a gun you go close to a man when there is no
need for it, you are a fool. Remember, one hand must
hold your gun which you cannot fire. He has two hands
free ; if he closes with you, you cannot use your gun.
Try this with an unloaded gun and see. We will illustrate
this point later when dealing with an armed man.

Rifles and Guns

The difference between a rifle and a gun is very real.
The rifle fires one bullet which will go a long distance with
great accuracy. The shot-gun fires a whole packet of small
shot, which spread out in a round pattern about two feet
across at 25 yards, so that anything passing through the
pattern will receive many shot, some of which may strike
a vital part. Beyond 50 yards, the pattern is so large that
very few shot will strike the object fired at, and those
shot, owing to their small size, will have lost their velocity
from wind resistance so that they do not penetrate. The
larger the shot the fewer there are of them, but the greater
the distance at which they are effective. Shot from 5 upwards
(6, 7, 8) are only effective against a man at close range,
not more than 30 yards. At 50 yards they would hardly

penetrate his clothing, though if they hit his face there would be a good chance of blinding him, or blood might run down into his eyes, rendering him unable to shoot with accuracy. Sizes from 4 downwards to S.S.G. are effective at 50 to 60 yards. The size recommended is "double-A" (A.A.). Buckshot is a loose term which includes all the large shot. In that sense it is used here. If you have cartridges loaded with small shot 5, 6, 7, 8, and do not wish the expense of buying others with large shot, just make a hole in the end of the cartridge and shake out the small shot. Buy large shot cheaply at the ironmonger's and load them through the hole and shake them down into place. When the cartridge is quite full, seal up the hole with paraffin wax.

Many of the fields of England are not more than 100 yards across and the hedges and banks give means of approach under cover, so that, if parachutists land in these fields anyone armed with gun and buckshot ought to be able to approach without being seen and deal with them effectively. In most parts of the country, except on the open downs, the failing light of the evening, or the uncertain light of early dawn, gives an advantage to the man armed with a gun and buckshot. The ·303 single bullet of the rifle can easily miss its target but the wide pattern of the gun should plaster it every time.

The use of the rifle will be taught by the commander of the Section or a military instructor, and Army manuals are published on the subject, so that there is no need here to describe the differences between the different patterns issued. A good deal, however, must be said about the sporting shot gun.

Carrying a Gun

When not in use, there are various ways of carrying a gun. Only two of these are really safe.

1. The gun can be carried resting on the top of the shoulder with the trigger guard uppermost, the barrels then point up into the air. If the trigger guard is downwards, resting behind the shoulder, the barrels are pointing at the head of the man behind you.

2. The gun may be carried with the stock between the upper arm and the body with the barrels pointing

downwards and forwards over the forearm. This position is sometimes made safer by opening the breech when the barrels point more directly downwards. This, however, is not recommended for night work where, if you stumble and fall, the cartridges might slip out without your knowing it. A noise is also made if the breech has to be closed quickly in an emergency.

Wrong Way   Right Way

Right Way   Wrong Way
Carrying a Gun

Warning. Perhaps the most comfortable way of carrying a gun is to rest the barrel in the crook of the elbow, while the thumb and fingers grasp the thin part of the stock just behind the trigger guard. This position is most dangerous, as the barrels are pointing directly at the person at your side. No one appreciates looking down loaded gun barrels. Do not carry your gun in this manner.

The rifle is provided with a sling to enable it to be carried easily and comfortably. On the Continent the same applies to the gun, but in this country no sporting gun has a sling. One should be made out of 2-in. webbing. It is slipped over the barrels, and the whole in the webbing stitched round buttonhole fashion. The other end is fastened to the thin part of the stock—not to the trigger guard. The gun can then be slung over the shoulder, carried on a bicycle, or when you have to swim.

Right Way   Wrong Way
Holding a Gun

Holding the Gun at the Ready

When holding the gun ready for use, the right hand grasps the thin part of the stock, the forefinger outside the trigger guard, the thumb on the safety catch on top. The palm of the hand should be comfortably at the side of the gun. The left hand should be at a convenient distance along the barrels. This distance will differ with individuals but is usually about the end of the wooden forepiece under the barrels. If the hand is too far forward, the barrels have a tendency to come up too soon, while if the hand is too far back the barrels are apt to sag. Barrels and stock should come naturally to the shoulder. The gun can be carried pointing directly forward, or pointing upwards diagonally across the body. The safety catch should always show the word "safe" ; when it is pushed forward, the word "safe" is hidden, and the gun can be fired. As the gun is raised to the shoulder, the thumb pushes the safety catch forward, the forefinger finds the trigger and the gun is fired. After practice the whole movement becomes automatic.

Aiming with a Gun

A gun is not aimed in the sense that a rifle is aimed. A rifle has a long range, and only one bullet ; it is therefore essential to be accurate. Calculations as to distance and windage are necessary and the sights must be carefully set. A gun is only used at short range and has no sights. There is a round dot at the end of the barrels of most guns but it is of no importance. A gun is pointed at an object and fired. If the object is moving quickly an allowance is automatically made as to the rate of movement—slow-moving objects can be considered as stationary.

If you point your finger at an object, you rarely point it in line with your eye, yet if you keep your hand still and move your head to look along your finger you will find it points accurately at the object. Try this and see for yourself. It does not matter from what position you point your finger, it will always point at the object.

That is just how you fire with a gun or a pistol, you point it and fire it and the charge goes where you pointed it.

As with every other calculated movement, practice is necessary to acquire facility, smoothness and accuracy. The novice, therefore, should lose no opportunity of putting the gun up to his shoulder and pointing at an object. Practice, however, should aim at accuracy rather than rapidity—that comes later. This practice can be carried out in a room where brackets or pictures can be aimed at. Firing is not so essential except to check the results of practice.

Stance for Shooting

In shooting forward, the feet should be comfortably apart, the left one slightly advanced. The weight of the body should be on the left foot, and the right heel just raised from the ground so as to enable the body to pivot round easily. When shooting upwards, the weight should be on the right foot with the left heel raised, this again allows easy and smooth pivoting.

Forward   Upward

Stance for Shooting

Getting over an Obstacle

When getting over a gate, hedge, or stile, or through a gap, get into the habit of opening the breech of your gun. Do not remove your cartridges. Sportsmen always remove their cartridges, but you are not after rabbits. If you remove the cartridges and put them in your pocket so as to have a free hand to get over the obstacle, then to reload you must fumble in your pocket, get hold of the right end of the cartridges and slip them into the breech and close it. This takes some time. It may be that as you are getting over or have got over, you may see an enemy, or what is worse, an enemy sees you. You are attracting attention by your movements and noise—he is loaded, you are not. An expert may be able to load his gun with rapidity, a novice cannot do so. Therefore keep your cartridges in place. This is war, not sport.

Care of the Gun

A gun is a delicate piece of mechanism though nothing shows on the outside. It deserves to be taken care of. Just remember, too, that many of the guns used by the Home Guard have been lent by private people to help the country and the least we can do is to take care of this property.

After a gun has been used it should be taken into its three pieces, the barrels, the stock, and the forepiece. The barrels should have an oily rag pushed down by a ramrod to remove the burned composition. When this has been done, another oily rag should be pushed up and down to polish the inside of the barrels. The stock should be wiped with an oily rag, and oil put into the lock round the triggers, at the hammer holes and into the movable mechanism. The forepiece should be oiled and the mechanism moved. Especially should this be done after a wetting. The gun is then put together and the whole wiped down with an oily rag. The springs should be released by pulling the triggers.

Warnings

1.   If you stumble and fall, and the ends of your barrels strike the earth, immediately on rising you must open the breech, remove the cartridges, and look through the barrels to make sure they are clear. The last inch or so of the barrels may have become choked with mud, sand or snow. If this has happened and the gun is fired, the barrels will assuredly burst with very injurious results to yourself. Do not forget this. To remove the block, take a stick and with the barrels pointing downwards, poke it in and out of the ends of the barrels, first one and then the other. If you hold the barrels upwards, the earth, grit, and small stones will fall into the breech and into the mechanism of the gun. Look through the barrels to make sure they are clear.

2.   Many patriotic ladies may hand in their guns and cartridges for use by the Home Guard. If they are 20 bore, refuse to have them in any Section. Sooner or later an accident will occur. A 20-bore cartridge will get among the 12-bore cartridges and will be loaded into a gun. Being small it will slip down the barrel out of sight and the gun will not fire. The breech will be opened and as no cartridge is seen, a 12-bore cartridge will be inserted. If that gun is now fired, the barrel will burst just where the left hand is holding it. The person firing it will lose his hand, probably his sight, and perhaps his life.

A 16-bore cartridge may be a nuisance but is not dangerous. Being small it will also slip down the barrel but only a little way. The block will prevent the insertion of a 12-bore cartridge, and, as the breech cannot be closed, the gun cannot be fired. First remove the 12-bore cartridge and ascertain the cause of the block. This must be removed by pushing a stick down the barrel and dislodging the cartridge, which should be returned with suitable compliments to its owner. The Section should be warned to look carefully over their cartridges to prevent a repetition of the occurrence.

Revolvers and Pistols

The revolver or pistol is a far more difficult weapon with which to shoot accurately and constant practice is needed to acquire accuracy. Few people in this country know anything about them and fewer can shoot straight with them.

The automatic pistol has been adopted by most countries, but we still largely use the revolver. When the revolver is fired there is considerable kick which throws it off its target, making it difficult to aim again quickly. With the automatic there is no kick as the recoil is taken up with throwing out the old cartridge and replacing it with a new one from the magazine, so that the automatic can be fired more rapidly and does not move from the target. A revolver holds six rounds, and can only be loaded slowly, bullet by bullet. The automatic may hold up to ten and is loaded rapidly with a clip.

In emergencies, when rapidity of fire is essential, the hammer of a revolver must be raised by squeezing the trigger, even though the effort involved in doing this will affect the accuracy of fire.

In taking careful aim, when there is plenty of time, the revolver should always be cocked by drawing back the hammer with the thumb.

Usually, an automatic is carried with ten bullets in the magazine and none in the breech. To load the breech the barrel is pulled back and let go.

To unload an automatic, remove the magazine and then pull back the barrel and let it go three times. Then you are sure that it is unloaded.

If the opposite is done and you pull back the barrel and see the breech empty and then remove the magazine, the automatic will still have a bullet in the breech as by the act of releasing the barrel, one is loaded from the magazine. If it is left now, an accident is liable to happen.

Using a Revolver or Pistol

When using these weapons much depends on circumstances.

If the enemy is unaware of your presence and within range raise the weapon slowly and take careful aim. If he is approaching you, immobility is essential so as to avoid attracting attention. Allow him to come close ; the closer he is the more deadly you will be. Most pistols throw rather high, aim therefore at his stomach. If the enemy has seen you and is going to shoot, spend little time on aiming. Fire and fire again ; if you can hit him anywhere you will upset his aim.

DEALING WITH AN ENEMY

Dealing with an enemy may appear to be a simple matter—but only at first sight. Ask yourself what you would do if confronted with an enemy for the first time in your life. You would find him a bit of a puzzle—not only a nuisance, but a serious danger. All your attention must be given him, or he will turn the tables on you, as you may learn to your cost. Nothing is more encouraging to a prisoner than to find that his captor does not know how to handle the situation. You want to give the impression that you are an old hand at it. It is just as well, therefore, to give the subject a little thought.

How are you going to deal with an enemy who has landed from parachute, or plane, and is in an easily-recognized uniform ?

Ask yourself what the enemy will do to you if you fall into his power, and the answer as to what we do to him becomes plain. He has no time to take you prisoner, and nowhere to take you. He has to get on with the job in hand, which is to press on and do injury or cause confusion throughout the countryside. There is only one thing he can do and that is to kill you. His ruthless behaviour to women and children, mowing them down with machine-guns and crushing them with tanks, and his general cruelty leave no room for doubt as to how the German soldier has been ordered to treat his victims.

Such then being the declared policy of the Germans, which they will certainly put into practice if they come here, they cannot complain if they are made to swallow a little of their own medicine. The answer then to the question as to what to do with the Hun soldier is to kill him or wound him as severely as possible. If he surrenders, it is a different matter.

So much for the open enemy, but there is the German disguised as a British soldier, or officer, and even as a staff officer, for the German does things thoroughly, and the higher the rank the more authority he can wield. There is also the Fifth Column man, a German agent in civilian clothes, just as dangerous as the soldier. The element of uncertainty makes this a difficult problem to deal with, and still more difficult to give advice about. The situations which may arise are so various and diverse that it is almost impossible to lay down rules. Only general principles can be given to guide the beginner as to what he should do and, more especially, what he should avoid doing. Beyond that initiative, intuition, and above all pluck and determination must be relied upon to get him out of a tight corner.

The Sections may at first have a very limited number of rifles and many will only be partly trained in their use. But most of them have a knowledge of shot-guns, especially if they live in the country, and anyone can easily be taught to handle them effectively.

What is written under the heading of "Firearms" should be studied carefully.

Typical Situations

The first situation, we will imagine, is where two men meet, each being armed with a gun

Let these two men meet suddenly. F. (friend) sees E. (enemy) first, and pointing his gun at him, calls on him to halt.

For the sake of illustration, I am going to make F. do everything he should not do, and will point out the mistakes made, but there will be nothing forced or unnatural in what will happen. I have known men lose their lives by doing just what F. is going to do now.

F. shouts to E. "Give me that gun." E. hesitates, sees he is covered and sulkily comes forward, holding his gun by the barrel, and gives it to F.

This seems quite satisfactory and straightforward, and if I were to ask which was the disarmed man, you would at once answer, "E. of course." That is where you would be entirely and absolutely wrong, and if you were F. you might be a dead man in half a minute.

Let us see what has happened. E. has approached F. and given up his gun, but he is now within springing distance of him. F. is holding his gun at the forepiece in his left hand, the natural place to hold a gun, and he has taken E.'s gun with his right hand. F.'s hands are occupied with holding two guns, neither of which he can use—he has actually disarmed himself and not the other man whose hands are both free. F. through ignorance has delivered himself to E. What a fool he has been ! Yet how naturally it has all come about. Now let us continue the sequel.

E., a dangerous and resolute man, on handing his gun

Friend F.   Enemy E.

F.   E.

to F., immediately clutches at F.'s throat with his left hand while he brings over the right with all the weight he can put into a blow straight to F.'s jaw. Down goes F..

c

and E. should finish him off without difficulty. But E. himself may still make mistakes which will reverse the situation in just as dramatic a way.

How is E. going to kill F. ? He may pick up a gun and shoot F. as he lies upon the ground. Then the battle is over, but if he does so he runs several risks. Let us see what they are.

1. The blow will have thrown F. upon his right side and taken E. slightly to F.'s left side quite naturally. In his haste E. will certainly pick up the nearest gun which will be the one fallen from F.'s left hand, and that will be F.'s gun and not his own, which was in F.'s right hand. The gun may be unfamiliar to him and not cocked and E. may have to fumble for the safety-catch, and then, when he fires it, discover that it was not loaded. "Rubbish," you may say, "how can a gun not be loaded in an emergency ?" Just ask the next sporting person you meet how often this happens and you will understand.

Let us hope that F. dodged, and the blow was a glancing one, and the knock-out was only temporary, and that F. recovers just in time to do the only thing possible. He must catch E. round the knees and bring him to the ground, and then it is anybody's fight.

2. E. may make another mistake. He may pick up a gun, and holding it by the barrels as if it were an axe, bring it down upon F.'s head, quite a natural and effective thing to do. He could not do anything more risky or stupid.

Suppose that gun is on cock as he strikes F.'s head, look where the barrels are pointing ! Try it for yourselves. They point straight into your abdomen. The mechanism of a sporting gun is so delicate that the chance of both barrels going off is almost certain. So that though poor F. is done for, E. also has found a sticky end.

Warning. In a fight of this nature, you should never kill by shooting. The reasons are quite sound. Your ammunition may be limited and you may need every round. Equally important—your opponent may have a confederate. A shot will put that confederate on the alert. He knows that someone is where the shot came from. He does not know what has happened, but he will endeavour to find out. You are ignorant of his presence.

The right course is to kill with the butt of the gun. Hold the gun by the barrels and forepiece and jab the butt

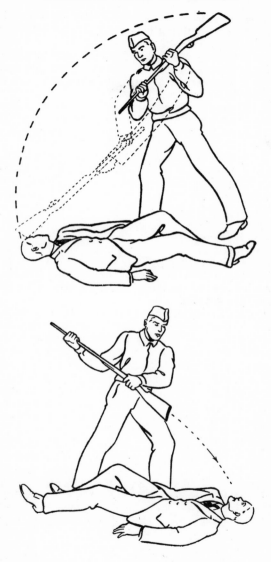

down sideways on to the skull of your opponent. If his head is on the ground it will crack like an egg, giving its owner a sure and painless end.

Having described what should not be done and its consequences, let us consider what should be done. The right course is more simple. Nothing goes wrong, and there can be no quickly alternating crises.

F. has the drop on E. and says "Throw down that gun." Down goes the gun. The next order is "Hands up." Then "Turn round." Then "Take four paces forward."

You have separated him from his gun and he cannot see what you are doing. Bear in mind you are never safe with a man looking at you, your attention must sometimes be distracted—then is his chance—look out.

You have taken his gun but you do not know that he is disarmed, he may have a pistol in his pocket. You therefore proceed to investigate. Walk up to his back and thrust the muzzle of your gun hard into the middle of his back, so that he knows it is there. You can then proceed to search him.

Warning. There is a simple rule always to be followed when alone and near a prisoner who is not secured. It is never to lose touch with him. Keep in contact with him with hand or firearm. Your attention may suddenly be distracted by someone, friend or enemy, bursting through the hedge behind you. You cannot help glancing to see what is happening. Knowing this the prisoner, even with his back to you, may turn in a flash and grapple. If it is an enemy who has come through the hedge, the end for you may be unfortunate. But if you are in contact with him, and if he makes any sudden movement you sense it at once, and your finger presses the trigger. If he makes

no movement rotate him at once to face the danger point, and look over his shoulder, using him as a shield.

Two men with guns meet a man with a pistol

In the next situation, two men with guns meet a man who has a pistol in his right-hand coat pocket.

We will suppose an enemy agent in civilian clothes, who is sneaking along a hedge with his hand in his right-hand coat pocket clasping an automatic, walks right into two men with guns, who, having heard him moving, are waiting quietly. He comes right out of his cover before seeing them, and there is no time for him to slip back as both are pointing their guns at him. He is ordered to put his hands up.

Here, again, I am going to make the two men do the wrong thing just to emphasize what you should not do, and to illustrate the possible consequences of the mistaken course.

The enemy, having put up his hands, stands still watching his captors and waiting for his chance. Remember, no risk

A.   B.   E.

is too great for a spy to take—if captured his fate is sure. His two captors are standing more or less side by side.

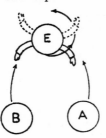

Looking at the prisoner whom we will call E. (enemy), the captor on the right we will call A., that on the left B.

A. now goes forward to search and disarm E., while B. covers him with his gun. As A. goes forward holding his gun in his right hand and leans across E. to get at his right-hand pocket, he partially shields E. from B. Now is E.'s chance. He drops his left hand over A.'s shoulder and clasps him tight, drops his right to the gun in his pocket. Holding A. as a shield he shoots at B. from his pocket. As his automatic has plenty of shots, B. coming to A.'s help is bound to be shot, after which E. shoots the struggling A.

If A. holds his gun in his left hand, his position is even worse as he must lean still further across E. to get at the wanted pocket, and his right hand will be caught between the two bodies. His left hand will be useless till he drops his gun which he cannot use.

Here, again, the tables have been turned simply by the ignorance of A. and B. and the resolution of E.

Let us see what A. and B. should have done.

No sooner have they covered their man than they should separate if they have not already done so. If they are close together and E. has his hand on his automatic in his pocket, he may risk pressing the trigger twice in rapid succession as he drops to the ground, chancing to get one or both of them. If A. and B. are separate he may get one but he will not get two as he has to turn, and split seconds count in this matter.

Having separated, the best thing to do is to turn E. round when he can be searched without difficulty.

If this is not done, then the right-hand man A. should stand still, and B. can go to the right-hand coat pocket

leaving A. with a clear line of fire. Having taken his pistol,
B. wants to get at the other pocket. Now if B. goes across
E., E. again will be shielded from A. and may make a fight
for it, especially if he has a dagger, a weapon now favoured
not only by the Italians but also by the Germans. B.
should avoid doing this. The proper proceeding is to stand
still and turn the prisoner round. Always turn him away
from you and not towards you : his front is his dangerous
side. With his back to you he cannot see if your attention
is diverted. With his back to you, you search him. First
his left-hand coat pocket, where spare ammunition is
usually kept, then his arm-pits where the American gangster
is fond of carrying his gun, then his hip pocket : feeling at
the same time for any belt to which a dagger might be
attached. Lastly, feel the upper part of his thighs, both the
outer side and high up in his fork. I knew an officer in
the Boer War who always carried a small revolver strapped
to the inner part of his thigh. He was taken prisoner by a
ragged Boer who made him take off his coat and then
ordered him to take off his riding breeches. The officer
began to obey, but while appearing to undo his breeches,
suddenly produced his revolver. He shot the Boer, dressed
again, and rode off on the Boer's pony.

It is just as well to do the thing thoroughly—so feel
round the upper part of the captive's boots. This is a handy
place to carry a sheath knife, much as the Highlander
carried his knife in his stocking. In a tussle even if your
arms are pinned to your side, you can lift your foot and
take your knife without your opponent knowing what you
are after.

You Wish to Disarm a Man Suspected of Having a Pistol

Here the situation is much the same as with the man
with the gun, except that the suspect may have his hand
in his pocket grasping his pistol. If possible, take cover
and watch him carefully to see what he is up to. Is he
spying things out, sneaking along, or hiding. Have patience,
there is no hurry. If you can do so unobserved, lob a small
stone into a nearby hedge and watch the effect the noise
has on him. The reason you must try and be certain is
that when you challenge him, you must fire immediately
if he hesitates to throw up his hands. Remember he has

only to press the trigger of his pistol and shoot you through his pocket. It is your life or his. You therefore take the best cover you can, moving with extreme slowness, and watching him all the time. If you are near a ditch, lie down among the grass and tall weeds, with only your head showing. Allow him to come well into the open away from any hedge or building before challenging him, otherwise he may dodge back out of sight before you can get him, especially if you are not a good shot. If he takes his hands from his pocket, then is the moment to challenge.

Your challenge must be "Hands up" in a loud voice. You fire if he does not at once obey. If he obeys, do not move but say "Turn round and do not look or I fire." He then cannot watch you rise. If he is near a hedge or a building it is a good plan to make him come five paces forward before you turn him round. The reason for this is that if he has a confederate some way away, you do not want the confederate to see what is happening.

If you have seen him signal, it is essential that he should come forward out of the sight of his confederate and you must act quickly.

You go forward and thrust your gun hard into the middle of his back and disarm him as just described.

If you have seen him signal, ask him if he is alone, you will then know if he is lying.

If there are Confederates

As a rule Fifth Column men work alone or in pairs so that one can vouch for the other. When there is no time to verify statements it is remarkable how successful this can be. It is very unlikely that there are more than three Fifth Column men.

Having disarmed one prisoner, if you hear others approaching do not lose your head and bolt, or they will all be after you led by your late captive who knows you are alone. Deal with him silently by jabbing the butt of your gun to the back of his head low down. He will drop stunned. You are now ready for the next man. If he is alone you can capture him in exactly the same way, especially if he does not know you are there.

If, however, you hear voices or the footsteps of more than one man, it is best to fire at the second man and then run forward to the gap in the hedge or to the corner of the building and take them as they come on. If you have dealt silently with the first man and shot the second, as you come round the corner you will probably see the one or two others making off and can pepper them as they go. Remember, that attack in such circumstances is by far the best defence. The enemy do not know how many you are. You want to find out how many they are. If you do not attack, you may find that both sides are needlessly running away from each other. Worse still they may chase you.

We have been dealing with Fifth Columnists. It may be different with German soldiers, but I do not think so. You are in your own country and should know every inch of it and therefore have a great advantage. It is for him to seek a hiding-place, not you. If you know the locality you should know where he is likely to hide.

While never despising your enemy, do not give him credit for very great reasoning power. He will not always hide in the best place—he will be a stranger and not know where to go—you may find him right in the open, where you would never expect to find anyone of sense.

Dealing with a Suspicious Visitor to the Hut

If you become suspicious of a visitor to the hut, it would be foolish to leave him alone in the hut while you take out another man of your Section in order to confide your distrust, even if this could be done without arousing suspicion. Even if there are several Section men in the hut you should not leave if you are the only one whose suspicions have been aroused. If you are fairly sure it is foolish to take risks. The visitor should be searched at once. How is this to be done safely and with the minimum of possible unpleasantness ?

With this contingency in mind every Section might have a test sentence which the man whose suspicions have been aroused might say in a way that all may hear, recognize, and so be warned that something is happening. It might be a sentence such as "Did any of you see the rainbow last night ?" Better still is a sentence which gives someone an excuse to go to the gun rack such as "John, have you cleaned your gun ?" "John" gets up saying casually, "No, but I will." He takes down his gun from the rack and comes to your side. This sentence should be altered from time to time and should never be divulged.

The stranger may not be alone, there may be two or more. The other patrol members should either take their guns or appropriate positions. This can all be done quietly, rapidly and effectively. Any movement of the suspected parties will be checked at once, such as the movement of the hand to the coat pocket. You can now quite politely say that you wish to search the stranger and proceed to do so. "John" is standing close by with his gun in his hand.

A Struggle with a Stranger in the Hut

This naturally leads on to the consideration of a struggle or fight in the hut, and what should be done. Some people's

ideas of a rough house are based on the experience of being chucked out of a music-hall or public house. This is something quite different.

If it is the sequel to what has just been described, everyone has been warned as to the possibility of trouble, and is standing ready. Now in a fight, especially in a house, you should never fire a gun if you can help it. When two people are locked together in a close struggle to fire is the most dangerous thing you can do. At close range, the shot from the gun acts as one ball and will go through the enemy's body and wound the arm, leg, or body of your friend on the other side.

In the hands of one who has been told how to use it, the

gun is a heavy and useful weapon even with no bayonet on the end. Thrust into a man's stomach, it will knock him out at once. When a struggle is taking place it should be bashed into the lower ribs with all the force possible. One or more of the ribs will be broken and all the breath knocked out of the body. It does not matter much which end of the gun is used.

There is another reason for not firing. One or more confederates may be outside, waiting some signal, and on hearing a shot they would at once come running in.

The question of confederates always crops up when dealing with a Fifth Column man ; remember this, and prepare for them.

A Hand-to-Hand Fight

In a hand-to-hand fight with a Fifth Column man you might be at a disadvantage as very probably you would not be armed ; your opponent might be. If you see clearly that a fight will take place, diplomacy is needed to postpone the actual onset till a favourable moment by which time you can hope to get hold of some weapon, lamp, syphon, poker. Having obtained your weapon, start the fight yourself by sudden attack.

"Twice armed is he who knows his quarrel just
But thrice armed he who gets his blow in fust."

If you can distract his attention, however momentarily, you may get just sufficient start to end the battle with a single blow, and a blitzkrieg is over. This may be done by looking beyond your man and nodding your head at an imaginary person, or saying, "Ah ! Jim, you are just in time." Your opponent is almost bound to turn round, or partially round, to see who is there. He does not want to take on two, and one of those behind him. As he turns, you let him have it with whatever weapon you hold.

If you can get no weapon and you are tolerably sure he is not armed, you can attempt to distract his attention, and then try a blow to the chin if you are a boxer and quick. If you are not quick do not try it, he may dodge just in time. Try and get him to turn to his left and give it him in the stomach ; no one can dodge a blow to the stomach. But remember, all your weight and good wishes go with that first blow. If he goes down as he should, you jump on him, not with your feet, but with your knees like an elephant. Come flop down on his chest with your knees. You knock all the breath out of his body and break his ribs.

If you have no weapon and you are attacked, you must have your wits about you. If he is the heavier man you will want them. Do not, however, be dismayed, weight has more influence in the ring than in a rough house. If you know what you want to do, and how to do it, you have a far better chance than a bigger man who has never thought it out, and just takes things as they come trusting to weight and strength.

Get out of your head the idiotic fights you see in the cinema where, without even appearing groggy, both sides in turn take blows that would put them to sleep not for the count but for a week. Each well-delivered blow seems to stimulate these gentry to greater efforts, and at last the hero wins. These are stage and not real fights.

What is your plan of action?—you must have one. It may be a life-and-death struggle and you know it. All right, keep calm. Remember it is a very difficult thing to kill a man with your hands especially if you do not know how. In a stand-up slogging match you will be beaten. If you do not think you can escape do not run away unless it is to get a weapon, the pursuer always has the advantage. You do not want to give him more advantage than he has.

Your safest plan, though you may doubt it, is to close with your enemy. He can then only give short arm blows while you prepare to knock him out. To do this, you should bend forward a little to get your stomach out of the way, put your elbows close together with your hands up in front of, and rather to the left of your face, and you peer round your arms at your opponent. By this means you protect your face from his right fist which he will try and get to your chin. Your head dodges to the right out of the way of his blow and you go in to meet him. As you close with him you separate your elbows, and your arms pass down on either side of his head and shoulders to just above his elbows. You lock your hands behind his back with your hooked fingers, a grip sometimes called a Lewis. Next you try to pin his arms to his side. You now hang on and fasten yourself to him by the strongest grip in your body—though you may never have used it as a grip before. You turn in fact to the primitive weapon of most animals

—your teeth. Take a big bite of the side of his neck as far back as you can get it, turn your head slightly so he cannot bite you, and bite as hard as you can. Any plan your opponent may have had will disappear with the pain and he will simply struggle to free himself. He cannot get his hands up to your throat or to your eyes, and he cannot get away. Meanwhile, you bring your left knee forward between his knes ; this is quite natural as you have leaned to your right and therefore your weight is on your right foot. His weight will be on his left foot and therefore he

cannot raise it from the ground, and there is no fear of his doing what you are about to do. Once your knee is between his, bring it up as hard as you can into his fork or crutch once, twice, or three times. You are sure to knock him clean out with a blow on the testicles. There is no surer way of doing this.

This whole manoeuvre takes some time to describe but in practice it is all one continuous movement which can be carried out naturally in a quarter of a minute. The fight is really over almost before it has begun. But you must know what you want to do before you close with your enemy : and do it quickly, deliberately, and thoroughly. You must not fail, and you must not let him know what you are trying to do before it is done and over.

You should practice this slowly with a friend, but be very careful of that knee ! ! !

Once he goes limp you can let him go and hasten his fall with your fist. When he is down crush him with your knees. How you finish him off does not matter.

Dealing with a Prisoner

The Home Guard must recollect that there are two very different classes of prisoner.

The first is the German soldier made prisoner in this country. He knows he will be treated with the honours of war. He will probably resign himself to his fate knowing that the chances of escape to his own country are small. The only exception to this being that if he has been sent out by a body of his troops, and knows where they are, he may take a chance of escape to rejoin them in spite of the risk of being shot. No liberties should therefore be allowed him.

The second class of prisoner is the soldier in disguise or the Fifth Columnist. He is a spy. Everyone knows the fate of a spy when caught. He must therefore take every possible chance to escape, no matter how risky it may be. The safest and best way to escape is for him to kill his captor ; it destroys the evidence, gives him arms, delays or prevents pursuit. Let it be impressed on the mind of every Home Guard that soldier prisoners are always awkward people, but that spy prisoners are very dangerous, as they must try to kill you to escape.

Once the prisoner is captured, searched, and disarmed, he should be marched off to the nearest police or military authority. A full report, in writing if necessary, should be made at the time, since his captor may be injured or killed later and unable to give evidence.

The following remarks apply to both classes of prisoner.

When marching a prisoner along to hand him over to the authorities, two armed men should always be sent with him. This is important as it lessens the risk of escape and makes the position much safer. At cross roads, gates, gaps, or corners, one can scout forward to see if the coast is clear, while the other gives his attention to the prisoner. Other enemies may be in the vicinity.

If you take and disarm a prisoner and are alone, make him march about ten paces in front of you with orders to look to his front and not to the sides or behind. If he

does not understand English, there are various ways of
making your meaning clear by pointing and threatening.

It is easy to take a prisoner along a road, but suppose
he is captured in a field. This makes a difference, for
you must take him to a road or path either through a gate,
over a stile, or through a gap. If he is taken in a house or
barn, you will have to take him through a door. All these
are places of possible danger, both from him, and from the
fact that you do not know what may be lurking round the
corner of these obstacles. Other enemies may be anywhere.

The Gate. Make the prisoner open the gate wide and
walk straight through and halt. "Halt" has the same
meaning in German as it has in English. Do not tell him
to turn left or right as he can then see you while you are
giving your attention to the shutting of the gate. If he
cannot open the gate, either by pretence or because it is
locked—look out ! It is quite possible that you might
lose patience at his fumbling and go forward to help him.
Do nothing of the kind, that is what he wants. Make him
get over the gate and stand with his back to you as before.
Then you examine the fastenings of the gate, and you will
know if he is playing tricks. If locked, you get over
yourself.

The Stile. Make him get over the stile and stand with
his back to you some ten paces away. Do not take your
cartridges out of your gun.

The Gap. At a gap he goes through first and walks
straight forward into the road or field. Look out he does
not bolt out of sight down the hedge. You then get through
the gap, but be ready, you may have to bend double to
get through.

The Door. Taking him through a door is a difficult
problem. Here you must get fairly close to him. If the
door opens away from you there is no trouble, but if the
door opens towards you, be on your guard ; or having
opened it, he may slam it in your face behind him and
bolt. By the time you have opened it he may be round
the corner, and out of sight. Or he may be waiting for
you as you rush round the corner and knock you clean out.
In this case, either you get close enough to control the door
with your foot, or you make him stand aside and open
it yourself. Always run wide round a corner when chasing
a prisoner.

Warning

Englishmen are prone to think that once a man is what they call "down", friendly relations can be established ; the German has different ideas.

Therefore :

Do not offer cigarettes.

Hold no conversation with him even on such a trivial subject as "Where are you taking me ?"

Do not on any account allow him to try and do you a friendly turn such as helping you over the gate, extending a hand at the stile, or holding back brambles at the gap. If he gets hold of your hand, you are disarmed ; you have your gun in the other and you cannot use it. He has one hand free ! Do not go near him if you can avoid it. It is much simpler if you have a revolver or a pistol which is a single-handed weapon, but recall the earlier warning about coming close to your enemy with a gun.

If you have taken his pistol, do not rely upon it if you are not familiar with the make, it may be at safety and will not fire when you press the trigger.

Searching a Prisoner

In searching a person suspected of Fifth Column activities care is needed in seeking clues to his true character.

He should be searched at once before he can dispose of anything.

Notebooks and letters should be preserved as they may contain references to other agents.

The name he gives should be compared with that on his linen. Examine the tailor's mark on his clothes and buttons.

Is his handkerchief unusually large ? Does he have several different coloured ones ? If so they are probably for signalling. Has the torch he carries different coloured glasses ?

Tin boxes should not be meddled with. They may be booby traps, the explosion of which would assist the escape of the prisoner. Germans are fond of such toys.

The lining of his clothing should be examined for papers. Note if he wears two pairs of socks ; under the soles between them is a favourite place to carry papers.

Everything should be tied up and handed over to the authorities.

D

Parachutists landing

The landing of troops both by plane and parachute has been developed and perfected by the Germans, and there is no doubt that they have attained a high level of efficiency in this manœuvre, as was seen in the Low Countries. From all accounts the mortality among the troops landed was high.

Parachutists, when they are in small numbers, will land during the hours of darkness or semi-darkness. They will collect together if they are to act as a force to seize any place, and prepare the way for others to follow ; or they may separate widely if they are to act as spies and saboteurs. They will probably lie quiet till daylight when they can mingle unobtrusively with those moving about the countryside. Anyone found moving about during the hours of darkness would be investigated at once. It is one of the great advantages of the Home Guard that they are all local people and can tell a stranger very quickly by asking local questions. They should have such questions thought out beforehand, sometimes it is difficult to think out the right questions on the spur of the moment.

If parachutists are seen to land in any district it is difficult to be certain that all have been rounded up. Every effort should be made to capture the lot. They are strangers in a strange land, for however well you may know a district, if suddenly dropped into a field you may not know where you are. Comparatively few of them can have been in the district before.

To find and capture them one must put oneself in their place. We must ask ourselves why did they come ? What do they want ? How are they likely to go about getting it ? When we can answer these questions we will know roughly their plans. In any case knowing our own neighbourhood we know the important military objectives in our district, and can guess what the enemy have come for, and what they will attempt to do. How they have planned to do it is another matter, but plans to frustrate certain obvious methods of attack can easily be prepared.

The first thing the enemy must do is to find out where they are ; and for this reason all place names and sign-posts have been removed. The Russian parachutists in Finland easily found their way about by means of sign-posts and the names of towns and railways stations. The removal of place names is no obstacle to the local inhabitants, and as motoring for pleasure has come to an end, there remain only those who come on business, for them it is very awkward.

In times of emergency patrol men or Home Guards will be posted at every cross and fork roads to direct the military. Care will have to be taken by frequent rounds of inspection to see that the patrol man has not mysteriously been replaced by a German agent posing as the friend of the patrol man who "has just gone off for a minute." In the meanwhile the traffic is being directed in the wrong direction.

The next information they will need will be to find out if there are any troops in the neighbourhood, their numbers, disposition and their nature, whether artillery, tanks, or infantry. No information should be given to strangers even when in uniform. Officers know quite well where to go to get information ; any one who asks you should be suspected, so take a good look at him to enable you to give information about him. Remember if he speaks to you over a hedge or fence it will be difficult to recognize him again as you have only seen his upper part. Go out and talk to him.

Food will be carried with these soldiers and may last for some days. They must be supplied with some money, this will probably be paper money and possibly forged. Perhaps this is the reason for the recent issue of new pound notes and possibly the old ones will all be recalled.

Spies will undoubtedly be dropped but they will not be the menace to us that they were on the Continent. There they could get back with their information in a way that is impossible here. The spies who are sending messages by secret wireless are probably here already. It is possible that spies may be dropped with small wireless sets.

Parachute Troops

It used to be thought that some thousands of feet were necessary to be sure that the parachute opened in time, but with the specially designed Eschner parachutes used by the Germans, troops can be dropped from as low as 300 feet. If they are dropped from a great height, the wind scatters them over a wide area, and it might not be easy for them to concentrate or even find each other. From low altitudes, however, they can be dropped in the space of one or two fields. Suitable arms are dropped in separate containers from which they can be collected. When dropped, the troops have only automatic pistols, and can easily be dealt with by anyone with a shot-gun.

Allied Airmen in Distress

Care must be taken to recognize members of the R.A.F. and allied flying forces who are compelled to descend by parachute.

The chief points to note are :

They will come down singly, or in twos, or threes, never more than six.

They will probably come down from a considerable height.

The plane may be seen and its markings recognized, or its crash may be seen or heard.

There must always be a difficulty in distinguishing between an enemy in distress and one of the R.A.F. Our airmen have a special pass, and they will not run for cover on landing. Special orders have been issued to the R.A.F. to help identification.

Uniform worn by Parachutists

The dress of the German parachutist has so far been as follows :

Over the uniform is worn a grey-greenish gaberdine overall with zips down the front. This is loose in the body, with short legs and full sleeves. It is held in the middle by a leather belt. The collar is loose, often worn open, and the tunic collar, with brown or yellow piping, bears the unit number. The steel helmet has no flat rim in front or behind, and is secured by two straps, one in front and one behind the ears, it may be camouflaged a sand colour. On the side of the helmet is the flying badge. High boots with rubber soles are worn, and the grey trousers fall over the tops something like plus fours.

Arms

The rifles in the containers are loaded ready for instant use. Every man carries a pistol. One man in five has a machine pistol. Æach man may have two egg-shaped grenades. Pistol ammunition is carried in pouches attached to the belt or in the pocket. Rifle ammunition is in twenty clips of five in bandoliers slung round the neck. Clips for the machine pistols, six clips of thirty rounds, are in a haversack, or in two pouches joined by a strap which is slung round the neck. Machine-gun cartridges are in a long belt to be fed into the gun. A rolled bivouac cape is hung from the shoulders above the belt at the back. Field glasses are carried by the machine-gun squads. Rations may be carried in pockets in the legs of trousers.

With all this equipment, the soldier cannot be expected to be very quick across country, and can easily be outdistanced by anyone lightly armed.

The following is a list of weapons and stores likely to be dropped to landed troops :

750 mm. mountain gun	Axes
2 or 3 inch mortar	Lamps
Machine-guns	Explosive capsules
Anti-tank guns	Fuses
Ammunition of all kinds	Spades
Field glasses	Wire-cutters
Portable radio set	Collapsible cycles
Hand grenades	Barbed wire
Smoke candles	Detonators

Landing

Parachutists land in parties of six, twelve, or even more. The planes can carry up to thirty men. They are dropped more or less in a straight line across country ; so that if one is seen to drop, a guess can be made where the others are likely to be, even if they are not seen to land—as we must suppose the plane is travelling in a straight line. Anyone finding a parachute in a field should report the matter at once. A look-out should be kept for burnt patches in fields and a search made among the ashes for pieces of rope which might indicate a burnt parachute. In the Low Countries they set fire to the parachutes on landing.

Warning

German soldiers, if dressed in their own uniform, are entitled to the privileges of soldiers, and should not be treated as spies. If captured, they should be handed over to the authorities as prisoners, and not shot out of hand. On the other hand it must be remembered that they cannot extend such privileges to soldiers and civilians resisting them. They are unable to take prisoners.

Troop Carrying Planes

Troop-carrying aeroplanes will only land on large flat spaces such as aerodromes, large fields, or open expanses such as the downs. But there are other places which must also be kept in mind such as race courses, golf courses, and straight stretches of arterial roads. Sands at low tide are good, and excellent cover is available in the sand dunes near by. Many of these places can be rendered unsafe for landing by felling trees, placing cement-filled barrels, carts, farm implements, or hay-ricks in the middle of fields, or by cutting ditches across them, or stretching wires across, especially across the roads.

The Public is so familiar with aeroplanes that little need be said about them and their capabilities. They have even learnt now that they can carry light tanks. To land troops in any force in this country with only their immediate necessities would take a huge number of planes. Even in the Low Countries only two or three thousand were said to be landed altogether, though in Norway many more must have reached their destination by this means in the course of time.

We can dismiss at once that an attempt will be made to invade this country from the air by planes alone. The Germans are not believed to have sufficient troop-carrying planes to do it.

*Troop Carrying Gliders

The measures above mentioned to render spaces unsafe for the landing of troops from planes have already been put in hand in many parts of the country ; but it should be noted that such measures are not effective against the landing of troops from gliders.

*Written by Oliver L. L. Fitzwilliams, who has held a German Gliding Instructor's licence.

The development of British gliding has been so cramped and discouraged that few people as yet realize its possibilities. Gliders to-day are far from being flimsy structures. Strong, useful machines can be built easily, cheaply and rapidly in sizes large enough to carry six or seven men fully armed and equipped.

The object of towing gliders would be to increase the carrying capacity of each transport aeroplane, and this is quite a practical proposition. It avoids the necessity for excessively large planes which are difficult, and expensive to build and, perhaps more important, it avoids the necessity for landing large numbers of planes quickly in a limited area.

The standard troop-carrying plane used by the Germans is the Junkers Ju. 52. This machine can carry up to thirty soldiers with their equipment, and has ample power to tow four gliders. If each glider holds seven soldiers, the total carrying capacity is fifty-eight, which is a very considerable increase. This is made possible by the increase in the total wing area of the combination for given weight and engine power.

The only adverse effect is an unimportant loss of speed, and a probable inability to fly in cloud or in conditions of bad visibility. The combination could not easily be manœuvred, but this is really no great disadvantage as the gliders are uncoupled before landing while, on the journey to this country, the transport fleet must rely upon fighters for its defence whether gliders are towed or not.

The gliders themselves are not very vulnerable to attack from the air, as they carry no inflammable fuel and contain little vital mechanism. Their construction is such that it would be difficult to cause a structural failure by machine-gun fire and, as Germany is so liberally supplied with pilots, that each machine might carry a second and perhaps a third pilot. Even if damage to the towing plane forced the gliders to uncouple over the sea the occupants would stand a better chance of survival than the occupants of most planes.

When released from a height of, say, 10,000 feet, gliders can be expected to travel about thirty miles, more with a favourable wind. Their silence will make their approach unexpected and the presence of soldiers in a neighbouring field might be the first indication of their arrival.

The landing of large numbers of gliders presents no problem. These craft land on skids which extend along the bottom of the body, and are so arranged that they prevent the machine nosing over when landing on rough or boggy surfaces, such as would prove fatal to planes attempting the same landing. Fields of standing corn are ideal landing places for such craft and would provide a certain amount of cover for the troops. Fields which have been obstructed as described above, or which already contain large numbers of gliders, still remain suitable landing-places. It should be noted that gliders are quite easily manœuvred and that, apart from a head-on collision with a solid obstruction, breakage during landing does not endanger the occupants. Germany is well supplied with excellent pilots, and in their hands, gliders can safely be handled in a manner so rough as to shock those who are only accustomed to aeroplanes. This is all the more important as gliders used in an invasion of this country would not be used again.

It is interesting to note that for the initial securing of bases, it may not be necessary for the carrying planes to be landed at all, since the troops carried by them could be dropped by parachute to reinforce the more fully equipped troops landed from gliders, the planes returning home for reinforcements at once. This means that large forces may be landed far from places where landing by heavy transport planes would be expected.

Observing Troop Landings

When air raid warnings sound, the civilians take cover, but the Sections should go at once to pre-arranged places from which a good view can be obtained—the hill top, the church tower, the top or upper windows of a house, or top of a haystack. If there is no telephone near one man should be ready to take a message to the nearest phone. The first warning should be sent off as soon as sufficient is seen to make a useful message. One containing more detail may be sent later. The patrols should always take writing material as a message may have to be entrusted to a boy.

The messenger should return to the observation post as soon as possible guiding others to the spot. If the observer has gone he should, if he can, leave a written message in a pre-arranged place to say where he has gone to. Communication can thus be maintained.

The church bells should be rung at once to alarm the countryside, so that every able-bodied man can arm and resort to the rallying point. Church bells should not be rung simply because they are rung in the next village. That would only cause confusion, but if the enemy approaches a second village, that village should ring its bells at once.

Touch should not be lost with the enemy, as it is only by watching their movements that their intentions may be gathered. They may make for a bridge to blow it up, and warnings should be sent as soon as possible. Bridges are often in exposed places and are themselves good observation posts. Soon it is hoped all bridges will be guarded properly; at present there is often a sentry standing on top of the bridge, but there is no one underneath!

The enemy will probably make for the nearest road to stop a motor-car or cyclist, so as to get to the nearest village to telephone false news, wreck the railway station or signal box, or set fire to the petrol supply if they cannot use it. For this reason it is wise to see what they are about before sending messages, otherwise the cyclist or motorist carrying the message may be the one caught. The first warning, however, should go off without delay.

The parachutist's most vulnerable moment is when he is landing or soon after, when he has only his pistol and has not yet collected his arms from the containers. The Home Guard can attack at this moment with rifles or, among small fields, with shot-guns with great effect. If you do not attack at once, do not let the enemy know that they have been observed, or they may become cautious. On the other hand, they may cast caution aside and make openly for their objective. If you do meet one coming along a hedge, remember the points laid down in the chapter "How to Deal With an Armed Man" and deal with him accordingly and silently.

If you have to fall back, edge a little to the side. You can watch better from there and are not so likely to be seen. Once firing has started and the enemy begin to take cover they should be delayed as much as possible. This can be done by lining the hedges, roads and lanes along which they are attempting to pass. When the military arrive the Home Guard can be most useful in guiding them to the right place, their local knowledge will mean a lot.

Troops on cycles are the most easily dealt with. Those in

cars are more difficult, but the driver should be aimed at. If it is the car owner who has been forced to drive it is hard luck ; but there is no other way of stopping a car ; firing at the tyres, radiator, or petrol tank, does not stop a car at once.

Possible Forms of Attack

Plans for the invasion of Britain will have been worked out with characteristic German thoroughness. An invasion will probably be preceded by a terrific bombardment of London from the air, so as to upset organization and disrupt means of communication. The invasion itself will probably be a combination of three forms of attack, by bombing planes and landings by sea and air-borne troops.

The first troops landed prepare the way for further reinforcements. Parachutists and troops landed by plane and glider will try and seize an aerodrome or flat space where more can be landed rapidly. The force might then try to capture a port where heavy guns, tanks, and other equipment can be brought ashore.

Their main object will be :

1. The seizing and holding of suitable landing-places.
2. The cutting of telephone and telegraph wires and the sending of false messages.
3. Attacking some town or village capable of being defended against attack.
4. Blocking roads, seizing cars, cycles and petrol supplies.
5. To infiltrate the country in disguise and to upset the machinery of organization.

BARRICADES AND BLOCK-HOUSES

Barricades, block-houses and fortifications are being erected all over the country very rapidly. They may consist of earth, sand-bags, stone, or brick. They are erected on roads, bridges, and strategic points.

On roads the barricades are meant to obstruct traffic and allow the vehicles and occupants to be checked and searched. When searching these people they should, if suspected, be taken a little apart, for if an owner-driver has been caught by Fifth Columnists and made to drive, he will say nothing if they are still in a position to shoot him. The barricades may be made in a primitive manner so as to be readily removed to allow our troops and convoys to pass through when necessary. They are best placed at corners or curves where traffic naturally slows up. Experience in modern fighting shows that they are most effective when two barricades are arranged halfway across the road from opposite sides, one being some ten yards behind the other. The barricade cannot then be rushed by a car. Permanent barbed wire defence can be placed at the side of the road to protect flanking fire. Such barricades are very effective in controlling traffic but are useless against troops.

To control troops more substantial block-houses are being built. These should be erected so as to command straight stretches of road so that anything advancing would be under fire for as long as possible. These block-houses must have a clear field of fire in all directions, so that they cannot be approached by an unseen foe along a hedge or wall or through a shrubbery. For this reason they should project back from the road into the field so as to be able to fire down both sides of the cover. Their site and construction is largely in the hands of the military authorities, but many such posts will be held by members of the Home Guard. Some defence of all Home Guard posts is being arranged and that is largely in the hands of the Home Guard themselves. A little imagination and attention to camouflage will greatly increase the strength, efficiency, and safety of these posts. This can easily be done by making false loopholes half-way up the walls, framed perhaps with pieces of board to attract attention and painted a dark colour internally. From a distance they will appeal real and attract the fire of the attacker. Above the top of the parapet a wire or string should be stretched from which reeds, grass, or small branches are hung down as a fringe, hiding the heads of those firing over the parapet and covering the real loopholes. This will cause no obstruction to the defender whose barrel will displace the obstruction as he looks along his sights, while it deprives the attacker of a well-defined target such as a bare loophole.

Wire along top.

Loopholes

False loopholes →

Loopholes

Loopholes are holes in fortifications through which fire can be directed against the enemy from behind cover. Only one rifleman can fire from each loophole. To allow a wide lateral range of fire an embrasure must be made and the wall cut away in front or behind the loophole. For the field of fire it does not matter on which side the wall is cut away. But if the embrasure is in front of the loophole, every bullet entering the space is liable to be deflected from the sloping wall through the loophole into the interior of the block-house. The bullet may be mushroomed, but the splinters will fly in. On the other hand if the embrasure is made behind the loophole any bullet not entering the loophole directly will be flattened against the wall at its side.

Most of our block-houses have been built with the embrasure in front of the loophole. A bullet may miss the loophole by more than a foot and yet be deflected through. The size of the opening should be so small that it would

be difficult to throw a hand grenade through it ; many of
the present ones are windows nine inches wide by six to
eight inches high. If the embrasure is on the inner side, a
handy shelf is provided for ammunition, a block of stone
should be kept there to block the loophole when it is not
in use.

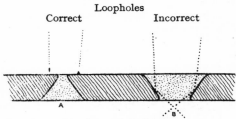

Interior of Block-house

Loopholes with an embrasure in front as well as behind
were introduced for machine-guns. They are not needed
for the Bren gun, which is supported near its muzzle.

If an embrasure is needed in front it might be stepped
or made flat.

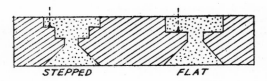

If the enemy is in strength and advancing along the road
he will have an advance guard in front of the main body,
possibly these will be on cycles. As soon as opposition is
met, word will go back to the main body who will deploy
into the fields on either side of the road, and advance as
quickly as posible. It is, therefore, a good plan to have
strong fortified points on either flank of the main block-
house. These will serve to delay the advance, as the enemy
will not know the strength of the defence. It will also have
the effect of making them deploy in greater width, and
make a longer detour if they are to get round to the rear
of the defence. This all takes time.

DEFENCE OF VILLAGES

It may be that the landed force may make for the nearest village or small town to use it as a base in preparation for a larger force following. It is an easier thing to prevent the taking of a village in the first place than to turn out troops who have once got in. When in they have excellent cover in houses, and can shoot from windows and doors where they cannot be seen. For this reason all roads leading into villages are barricaded. The Home Guard draws its members from every village and the villagers themselves should be instructed what to do in the case of an alarm being sounded by the ringing of the church bells. They should also be instructed what to do in case of hurried evacuation.

Delaying the enemy is of paramount importance in order to allow the military to arrive. The Post Office should be informed at once so that they can summon help. Just as it is important to keep communication with the men who have seen the landing and who are watching the subsequent movements of the enemy, so it is important for the village to keep in contact with the outside world. The names of those who own a motor or even a pedal cycle should be known. They may be used as messengers should the telephone and telegraph wires be cut.

The success of troops landed from the air depends on two things—surprise and the rapidity of their movements.

Surprise can only be countered by a constant look-out kept day and night, and by everyone being prepared, that is, knowing what they have to do in case an alarm is given, and doing it without hurry or excitement. This entails a lot of organization most of which will never be called into action. Landings will only be made at certain places, but as we do not know which those places will be, all should be prepared. Every village should know just what it is expected to do. This means that every inhabitant should be spoken to personally and his duty explained to him. I wonder in how many villages this has been done.

We have been Warned

Those villages and small towns near ports, open spaces, such as the downs, near factories, and points where communications are important, such as Berkshire and Buckinghamshire, through which run the main arteries of traffic by road and rail, linking up the East and West parts of the country, are the places most likely to be called upon.

The rapidity of movement of the enemy must be limited by delaying and obstructing his movements by blocking the roads, firing from cover behind hedges on his flanks, and defending every strong point.

It cannot be too fully emphasized that the defence of the country is the business not only for the Forces, but of everyone from the highest to the most humble. Vital information may first come from a small farmer who sees the landing. Most efficient work may be carried out by the village shop-keeper who helps to block the road near the village or helps to screen the village street. No offer of help should be spurned, no effort should be obstructed or despised.

While preparations are being made to keep the enemy out of the village, preparations should also be made to resist them on their entry. Their field of fire down straight streets can be curtailed by hanging sheets, blankets or rugs from ropes across the streets at suitable points where a good field of fire can be obtained by the defenders. This can even be done under fire if people know how. A small weight can be thrown across with string attached by means of which wire or rope with carpets, rugs, etc., are already attached and the whole drawn up to the first-floor windows. Even a tank has to halt at such an obstacle as it cannot see what is on the other side. This prevents the streets being swept by machine-gun fire and makes sniping impossible. At the same time the arrival of relief troops, and movements of people beyond the screen, cannot be seen.

All doors of houses and sheds should be bolted and locked so that the enemy cannot dodge in under cover but must lose time in breaking open doors and windows while the defenders are shooting at them. Every household should have some scheme of defence and all can do something to help, even small duties such as locking the front and back doors, hiding the food, locking the cycle in the shed, all help. The authorities have asked every manufacturer and large shop-keeper to organize his establishment and appoint a commander and a second in command, and tell off the employees for special duties. It is to be hoped that re-hearsals for this and for village defence will soon be held to teach everyone his duties. There is nothing like a little drill. If every town and village is organized success by an invading force is impossible.

It all rests with the spirit and the energy of the people of this country—the women equally with the men. If we can deal with the small forces as they are landed no large force will be able to form.

END